THE END OF
FIERY SWORD

Adam & Eve and Jesus & Mary

EMMAUS
ROAD
PUBLISHING

Steubenville, Ohio
A Division of Catholics United for the Faith
www.emmausroad.org

Emmaus Road Publishing
827 North Fourth Street
Steubenville, Ohio 43952

Library of Congress Control Number: 2014952989
ISBN: 978-1-63446-003-3

Design and Illustrations by:
T. Schluenderfritz

Nihil Obstat: Rev. James M. Dunfee, *Censor Librorum*
January 24, 2014

Imprimatur: Jeffrey M. Monforton, Bishop of Steubenville
January 24, 2014

The *nihil obstat* and *imprimatur* are declarations that work is considered to be free from doctrinal or moral error. It is not implied that those who have granted the same agree with the content, opinions, or statements expressed.

THE END OF THE
FIERY SWORD
Adam & Eve and Jesus & Mary

MAURA ROAN MCKEEGAN

Illustrated by T. Schluenderfritz

Do you know about Adam and Eve?
About Jesus and Mary, too?
Two are from the Old Testament,
Two are from the New.
Their stories are the Word of God,
Their messages are true;
But when you see them side by side,
A hidden part comes through.

Now take a closer look
At how their histories are told:
See the Holy Spirit work
As mysteries unfold.
Find the buried treasures
That the Sacred Scriptures hold;
Let the New unlock the door
To secrets of the Old!

*"The New Testament lies hidden in the Old, and the
Old is unveiled in the New."* —SAINT AUGUSTINE

In a garden called Eden
God created a woman
without sin.
Her name was Eve
And God made her to be
the first mother
On the whole earth.

1

In a town called Nazareth
lived a woman
who had never sinned.
Her name was Mary
And God chose her to be
    the most blessed mother
On the whole earth.

2

A serpent tempted Eve
And told her
That if she disobeyed God's law,
She could be as wise as God.

An angel visited Mary
And told her
That if she obeyed God's will,
She would conceive the Son of God.

4

Eve ate the fruit
That God told her not to eat.
She said no to God,
And committed the first sin.

Eve gave her husband Adam
Fruit from the forbidden tree.
Adam ate it, and then blamed Eve
    for his sin.
Because of Eve's disobedience,
Her children and the whole world
Sinned against God, too.

Mary accepted the fruit
That the Holy Spirit placed in her womb.
She said yes to God,
And never sinned.

Mary told her husband Joseph
About the fruit of her womb.
Joseph decided to protect Mary
    from shame.
Through Mary's obedience,
Her child, Jesus, came into the world
To take away sin.

When Eve tempted Adam,
He ate the forbidden fruit.
In the Garden of Eden,
Adam hid from God.
He was afraid,
Because he had not done God's will.
God came looking
        for him in the garden.
Adam betrayed God,
And now Adam
        was going to die.

8

When Satan tempted Jesus,
He ate nothing at all.
In the Garden of Gethsemane,
Jesus prayed to God, His Father.
He was in agony,

But He was ready to do
    His Father's will.
Judas came looking
    for Him in the garden.
Judas betrayed Jesus,
And now Jesus
    was going to die.

In their sin,
Adam and Eve were banished from the garden.
God sent angels called cherubim
And a fiery sword
To guard the way to the tree of life.

11

In His obedience,
Jesus remained in the garden.
God sent an angel to comfort Him.
Jesus told His companion not to use a sword
To guard His life.

12

Adam made himself clothes
To hide his shame.
In the middle of the garden,
The forbidden tree held the cause of his sin.
Because Adam said no to God, his Father,
All human people would die.
God said Adam and Eve could not eat
From the tree of life
Or live forever with Him.

13

14

Jesus was stripped of His clothes
To bring Him shame.
In the middle of two sinners,
The wood of the Cross held the world's sin.
Because Jesus said yes to God, His Father,
His people no longer had to die.
Jesus said they could eat His Body,
The Bread of Life,
And live forever with Him.

15

16

When Adam and Eve died,
The gates of Paradise were closed.
But God had a plan
To open them again
Because He loved His people.

When Jesus rose from the dead,
The gates of Paradise were opened.
Jesus fulfilled God's plan
To open them again
Because He loved His people.

18

Author Biography

Maura Roan McKeegan earned her bachelor's degree in elementary education and spent five years teaching elementary- and middle-school children. While studying theology at Franciscan University of Steubenville, she was especially drawn to biblical typology. "I thought how great it would be to place Bible stories side by side, so that children could see the connections between the Old and New Testaments," she says. Maura grew up in Potomac, Maryland, and now lives in Steubenville, Ohio with her husband Shaun and their four children.

Illustrator's Biography

Ted Schluenderfritz is the illustrator of several books including *A Life of Our Lord for Children, The Book of Angels,* and *Darby O'Gill and the Good People.* He is a freelance graphic designer and the art director for *Catholic Digest* and *Gilbert Magazine.* He lives in Littleton, Colorado with his wife Rachel and their six children. You can view more of his work at www.5sparrows.com.

CPSIA information can be obtained
at www.ICGtesting.com
Printed in the USA
BVIC01n1529030316
438883BV00002B/2

* 9 7 8 1 6 3 4 4 6 0 0 3 3 *